MODERN HERO

Through Faith and Perseverance:
How I Became a Cool Smart Kid

Nahjee Grant

Printed in the United States of America

For more information please visit:

www.nahjeegrant.com

Also by Nahjee Grant

Newie (2013)

Aron's Adventures (2013)

Newie: Big City Dreams (2014)

Believe in Yourself (2014)

Aron Goes to the White House (2015)

Journey of the Cool Smart Kid (2016)

Aron Runs for Class President (2016)

Where Did My Dream Go? (2017)

Dedication

To my father, my first hero.

To my mother, for her love, guidance, and faith in me.

To Principal Marcia Hockfield for giving me the opportunity to get it right, because you didn't have to give me a second chance.

To President Barack Obama for having the audacity to run for president of the United States and inspire a young man from Ardmore to pursue his dreams.

- Nahjee

Everybody wants to reach the top but nobody
wants to climb the mountain.

Joseph Grant

Table of Contents

Acknowledgements

Edwin Hunter for your love and support.

Jill Fishman and Chris Gagnier for your mentorship and support of this book project.

Cathy Fiebach for hosting my first independent bookstore signing at Main Point Books.

Rhenda Fearrington for taking a chance on me and hosting my first Barnes & Noble book signing.

There are not enough words in the English-language dictionary to describe how appreciative I am of Lorraine Carter from AARP Experience Corps for everything she has done for me.

I want to acknowledge and thank everyone who has ever bought a copy of any of my previous books, donated their time or money to my nonprofit organization, and encouraged me to stay on the right path.

Introduction

From middle school through my first year in high school, I was not a very good student. I slept through most of my classes and hardly ever did my homework. My mom, who always tried her best to encourage me, asked if I wanted to be a Cool Smart Kid or a Cool Dumb Kid to motivate me to get my act together.

The path I was on was leading me to no good. I knew that I could do better and knew I had a higher purpose.

I chose to be a Cool Smart Kid.

The Cool Smart Kid was confident, intelligent, fearless, and focused on achieving goals.

We all know the most famous superhero in the world, Superman, had his alter ego, Clark Kent, who allowed him to blend into being human on Earth.

2

The Cool Smart Kid became my alter ego to stay focused, learn, and study in a more disciplined way, so I could be the best student I could. It allowed me to draw upon qualities necessary for my growth, and eliminate those causing me to fail.

Today I use the same qualities to inspire all children regardless of socioeconomic status, race, or gender, to reach their potential. Sometimes I feel like I don't have these qualities, but the Cool Smart Kid inside me knows exactly what to do. When I am in character, I can embrace the qualities I need to succeed.

In 2016 I wrote a children's book titled *The Journey of the Cool Smart Kid*, a story about my academic struggles in school and how I was a very unmotivated student, eventually flunking out of 9th grade. My intention for this new book is to shed some light on lessons learned and some of the character traits I developed during those years, and how relevant they were throughout my journey. I dug deeper into some of the struggles I had to overcome during my childhood and teen years that helped shape who I am today.

And lastly this book is for anyone who thinks they are not that cool, or brave, or confident. I want you to become a Cool Smart Kid and allow yourself to call upon your strong and fearless self to bring to light the qualities in you that are ready to shine for the world to see.

Chapter 1:

Childhood and Early Life

I'm from Ardmore, Pennsylvania and I'm very proud of growing up on a street called Sheas Terrace, where my great-grandparents and every generation since, lived. It's a small but lively street and every resident was African-American. Living in Lower Merion Township – which was predominately White – made for a very unique experience. Everyone looked like me and shared similar values and culture, but then you'd go to school and be the only African-American in the classroom and have to deal with cultural differences. Living in Ardmore and growing up on Sheas Terrace was a lot of fun. I had a lot of friends growing up and I played four sports. Even if you were not an immediate family member, everyone in the neighborhood was a part of your family, helping you grow and learn and teaching you valuable life lessons that I still use today.

When my friends and I were too young to leave our street by ourselves to go to the park and play, we nailed milk crates to the light pole to use as basketball nets. Sheas Terrace was a dead end street, and there was a field on the other side of a gate that closed off the street. The field was strewn with trash, broken glass, and dead animals but we made the best use of the space to wrestle and play countless hours of football.

I went to Penn Valley Elementary School, which was an interesting experience because I came from south Ardmore, and being in a neighborhood where you have a very diverse community and then going to a predominantly White elementary school and being the only young Black boy in your class was a very uncanny experience at first. As I made new friends I would often be invited to birthday parties and sleepovers. I had to learn how to interact with kids outside of my race and neighborhood. A lot of my classmates lived in wealthier areas inside Lower Merion and it would amaze me to see the size of their homes and hear about their experiences during family vacations traveling the world. I enjoyed school very much; I played a lot of sports and enjoyed art and music.

In first grade I created my first storybook, a short story about my favorite basketball player in the '90s, Michael Jordan, and I still have that book with me today as a reminder of how creative I was back then and how creative I can be today.

In second grade I played the clarinet and learned quickly that I was not very good at it – which my mom still reminds me today – but I gave it a try. That was one of my earliest lessons that when you try something you'll figure out if you're good at it or not. I learned that the clarinet was not for me, so I moved on.

When I was in the second grade, a substitute teacher who happened to work at a church a few blocks from where I lived asked the class to let her know if they knew anyone who would be interested in helping to clean up and work at the church. While all of my classmates were doing their work I walked over to her desk and confidently mentioned that my dad cleans churches. I wrote down our home phone number and she promised to give him a call.

A few days later when I made it home after school my dad gave me a big hug when I walked in the door, and took me out for ice cream. He said the teacher called and hired him to clean the church. I had the courage to speak up for my dad when I had the chance, and I was happy to see him get the job.

Outside of school I played basketball for the Malvern League with a few of my friends from the neighborhood. I remember a friend of mine who lived across the street was going to tryouts. I had no interest in playing on the team but I went with him and I sat on the sidelines to watch.

While the other kids were trying out, I was asked to come on the court to play and I made the team as well. The team was called the Rockets and we won the championship that year.

I played football in fifth grade; it was the first year that the team was formed and we called ourselves the Ardmore Panthers. I was a starting running back and at the time one of my favorite players was Barry Sanders who played for the Detroit Lions, so I took his #20 and imitated his running style. It was a very fun experience to play with a lot of my friends and we bonded during that year. I remember we were misplaced by age brackets, so we would play teams that were twice our age and our size, but it took a lot of courage and fearlessness to still play. Before the game we would look at the other team and see that they were much bigger in size but we played anyway and we had a lot of fun. At times we got hurt but we were proud we were able to stay in the game from start to finish.

I was also interested in hockey. I was a very good rollerblader when I was younger, and my dad found a hockey net and bought me roller skates and a hockey stick. The net became our entertainment when we were not playing basketball and my friends and I would play hockey after school.

One year my parents decided to sign me up for a Main Line hockey league at the YMCA. I quickly learned that playing on a team and following game rules was much different than street hockey. I enjoyed playing in the hockey league for one year before moving on.

I played for Lower Merion Soccer Club. My dad would take me to every game. I remember when I scored my first goal — dad had to run to the car to get something and I was jumping up and down with excitement and I looked on the sideline but there was no one there. When he came back I told him that I scored and he got all excited but also a little disappointed that he hadn't been there to see it. I had a lot of fun on the soccer team that year, and shared valuable time with my dad.

One of the proudest moments of my childhood was being a Boy Scout. My mom and dad signed me up and initially I did not want to be a Scout because scout meetings were every Saturday and I wanted to play with my friends every Saturday. But my mom was adamant that I be a Scout and pursue interests away from some of my friends and do something larger than myself, like being involved in the community. And I ended up enjoying it very much and learning a lot of life lessons and values during my time as a Boy Scout.

I will never forget marching in a parade for the first time as a Scout, which was the annual community Memorial Day parade, a very large event. I got to march next to my grandfather who was a Korean War veteran. He rode in a van carrying veterans throughout the parade and he watched me as I performed my steps.

I will always remember that moment and see the proud look on his face when I wore my uniform. I learned a lot about leadership and about having the courage to try new things. All of the values and life lessons I learned during Scouts carried with me throughout my life when they were most needed.

When I was 10 my parents divorced and I barely reacted to the split. They did their best to explain to me that their breakup was not due to me, but because of differences between them. Once my dad moved out I was fortunate that he did not move far away and I was able to see him on a weekly basis. I did miss him a lot; it was weird not having him around the house anymore. My grandmother passed away the same year and my mom was truly devastated by the loss of her mother. And even though Mom and I were going through changes at home, and dealing with a loss in the family, we became even closer and I took care of her just as much as she took care of me.

Since my dad did not move far he would make an effort to pick me up every other weekend to stay with him. On our way to his house he would stop at the church he worked at to finish cleaning. No matter how tired I was, my dad wanted me to learn the value of hard work and made me help him clean the church with a duster and broom. Afterward, we would pick up pizza and go home to relax. Oftentimes my friends would join me for the weekend and my dad would take us to places like the arcade or go-kart racing.

My dad did the best with what he had. There were times he would take my friends and me to a fast food restaurant and we all had to share Happy Meals because he did not have enough money to buy one for each of us. Whenever we asked for seconds he would famously say, "Drink your juice, then you'll be full." After a few gulps of juice I would always lose my appetite to eat. I was always angry when I didn't get another burger but it taught me a priceless lesson to never waste food and be grateful for what I have right in front of me.

Chapter 2:

Middle School Years

I went to Welsh Valley Middle School, which is the only school in our school system with an open campus. You have to walk outside to get from class to class so during the winter you have to make sure you are bundled up and warm, and during the warmer days you don't mind being outside and getting some fresh air. We had recess in between the buildings in the open courtyard. I remember a couple of my friends who also loved playing basketball were frustrated that we couldn't play the game outside because there was only an indoor gym. Every time we would see our vice principal we would ask him to find room in the courtyard to build a basketball court, and he would tell us a "maybe" and "we'll see," but we kept the pressure on. One day he finally said yes and the following year there was a half-court basketball court outside and we were able to play outside and have our own space instead of waiting for others to clear space in the gym.

I still saw my father all the time in the neighborhood and on the weekends at his house. But the pain of not having him in my life full time caught up with me by seventh grade. My way of reacting was closing everybody out including family and friends. I stayed in my room to escape the world.

I didn't care about anything at that moment in my life and my grades began to reflect my new attitude. I started to fail a few of my classes. When I applied myself I would do well but I rarely put 100% into my schoolwork or studying. My mom tried to get tutors and would always encourage me, but I didn't listen at all. Seventh grade is also the first year you can play sports for the school and I was really excited because most of my friends wanted to play, too. I made the team but shortly into the season my grades began to progressively get worse, specifically in math and biology, and I became ineligible for the team most of the season due to poor grades. I applied myself a little bit but it was never, ever, good enough.

My teachers would post our grades every week on the classroom door next to our student ID numbers, so only the student would know whose grade they were looking at. Every Friday I looked at the grades and saw an F. I would plead with my teachers every week to let me off the hook, hoping that my charming smile and funny jokes would win them over, but it never happened.

I remember this was the same year Kobe Bryant would get his high school jersey retired at Lower Merion. My uncle was a custodian at the high school at the time and hooked me and my dad up with tickets to see the ceremony. As we drove to the school it felt like Kobe had brought Hollywood to Ardmore. There were bright lights flashing in the sky and music blaring through the speakers and everyone in attendance dressed up like they were at a premier of a new movie.

My dad and I took our seats. I was mesmerized by the giant men at the other end of the stage who were towering over everyone in the gym. I had never seen NBA players in real life until Kobe's teammates joined him. Right before the ceremony began, there were two guys sitting in front of us debating Kobe's high school career and one of them said there's a kid in Ohio who is going to be one of the best players ever. He was either a fortune teller or figured out time travel and knew the future. I wonder if that kid, LeBron James, ever became a good NBA player? Anyway, the ceremony began, and the cheerleaders lined up from the gym entrance to the stage. The voice on the loudspeaker announced Kobe's high school accomplishments and he walked through the crowd making his way to the stage. My dad knew I was a fan of Kobe, and Dad used Kobe's success as a way to motivate and encourage me, saying that if he can do it, I can, too.

As he made his speech I looked to my right and I saw my school basketball team sitting together on the bleachers wearing their uniform jackets. Even though I was ecstatic to be there with my dad, I felt bad knowing I could have also been there with the team if I were a better student.

Once the season was over the only incentive to improve my grades was the class trip to Virginia, and I really wanted to go. My homeroom teacher made it very clear that if any student was not doing well in class they would not be eligible to go on the trip.

.

I also had to endure the lunch detention walk of shame every week. Since the school was an open campus you had to walk outside to get to the different buildings. If you fell behind in your school work, teachers would make you skip recess and spend the period in class making up the work. It felt like I barely got the chance to play outside during lunch because I was in detention every week. Since I had to walk outside from the cafeteria to the next building I would take my lunch tray and walk past all of my friends as they were playing outside. I would hear things like "There goes Nahj again!" "Man, you're in prison again for recess?!" yelling jokes and making fun as I dropped my head in shame every time.

There were some classrooms where I could see the outside courtyard and watch everyone play while I was stuck inside, the worst feeling in the world to me at the time. I would switch detention classes that I was failing in from math, to reading, to biology every other week. I used my friends' words as motivation to push through enough to improve my grades and eventually go on the trip.

My poor academic behavior spilled into eighth grade and I ended up just as uninspired as the year before. I often got asked by my parents if was I hanging out with the wrong crowd, and the answer was no. I played with my best friends from the neighborhood, but I was always different in the sense that I was always doing my own thing, never really doing what the crowd was doing; we really just had similar interests and all grew up together. I tried out for the basketball team again and the coach made it clear that I did not have a great chance of making the team, already due to my poor grades, and ultimately didn't make the team. This was a crushing blow not only because I really wanted to play, but because I had nothing to look forward to for the rest of the year except our end-of-the-year class trip to Six Flags.

The only way I could get motivated to complete my schoolwork was to use the class trip as a reward for improving my grades, and I passed by just enough to graduate middle school.

Outside of school I was a huge fan of BMX. Dave Mirra was my favorite rider and my dad bought me his signature bike, the Mirra Haro 540. My older cousin was a talented rider and I learned a lot of tricks from him. I studied the videos he had in his personal collection and I dreamed of one day being as talented as him. I was ecstatic when the X Games came to Philadelphia in 2001 and 2002. I had the opportunity to meet my favorite riders and watch a lot of great performances with my family and friends. By the time I approached high school, my love for BMX began to fade and I developed a new interest in street cars after watching the *2 Fast 2 Furious* movies.

Chapter 3:

High School Years

When I entered high school I remember my mom saying, "You're in the big leagues now, and if you thought it was tough in middle school you better get your act together in high school." I brushed off her comments because I thought I knew everything. The only thing on my mind at the time was playing basketball and wearing the maroon and white jersey Kobe wore. During the first week of school I brought home a booklet with all the extracurricular activities the school had to offer. My mom encouraged me to choose a few in the book that would interest me. I gave her the side-eye as I was checking my phone. "None of these things are cool; who wants to play chess after school when you can play basketball?" I used the booklet as a basketball and tossed it in the trashcan while sitting on the couch.

Looking back now I think it would have been the right choice to explore the options the school had to offer but I also believe getting what I deserved for dismissing it taught me lessons I never would have gone through in drama club or band.

For the first few months my grades weren't so bad, but I had the same attitude I had in middle school and it got even worse by the winter. My one and only dream for the year came true as I made the freshman basketball team.

This dream, however, was very short-lived as my disdain for school grew greater and I became academically ineligible most of the season. The incentive was to maintain a 1.5 grade point average, which is a pretty low bar; I assumed you could average a C in every class and be fine.

My experience playing basketball freshman year consisted of watching the team from the bench and practicing after school, knowing I had no chance of playing. Once the season ended my bad behavior in class became composed of sleeping in class, asking to go to the bathroom and not returning that day, leaving school earlier than I was supposed to. I seemed to find my way to detention weekly for failing to turn in my homework and I became such a regular in the principal's office that the secretary and I became good friends.

I was never the kid to get in trouble for being a troublemaker. All the adults would scratch their heads and make similar statements, such as "Nahjee, you're the nicest person I ever met, and you're always smiling. I just don't get it—how are you always failing?"

The summer after ninth grade I started my first job. I worked as a counselor at a summer camp where I used to be a camper myself. Serendipity Day Camp was heaven on earth. As a camper, I looked forward to it every summer and never wanted to leave and go back to school. Everything I needed was at my fingertips all summer long: girls, sports, the outdoors. Now as a counselor, I could make money, be in a familiar environment, and enjoy the summer.

Two weeks before school started, I received a letter in the mail, around the same time all students receive their school packets that detail who your teachers are and what supplies you will need. The letter stated that after further review I was not eligible to pass ninth grade. How do you tell someone two weeks before school starts you are not eligible? Ever heard of summer school?! I frantically called my mom at work, and was so upset by the news that I rode my bike to school hoping I would find someone at the administration building who could give me answers. Anybody! How could they hold me back in ninth grade? Shouldn't someone have told me earlier in the summer? No one was there and I returned home, dejected.

On the first day of school I brought this to the attention of the ninth-grade principal and she scheduled a meeting with the tenth-grade principal. I sat in the meeting by myself, my parents not present, so I had to defend myself. The tenth-grade principal had a reputation for putting down students and offered no wiggle room for sympathy, stating, "You couldn't do the work last year; what makes us think you can improve yourself this year?" adding, "You might as well stay back. It's only a year and you won't be too far behind your class." I immediately rejected his offer. He had no faith in me and I would never accept staying back another year under any circumstances.

Once the meeting was over I went back to the ninth-grade principal's office. She gave me an ultimatum and lifeline that I will never forget—she said that if I pass the first half of the school year with no failing grades she would put me in tenth grade for the remainder of the year. But if she saw any failing grades, she would keep me in ninth. I didn't want to be in that position but I was sure happy that I was offered a second chance to improve my grades. I accepted her offer, finished the school day and shared the news with my mom when I got home.

During our conversation she said something that still to this day I will never forget. She said, "Do you want to be the Cool Smart Kid, or the Cool Dumb Kid?" And she asked me if wanted to graduate with my friends or with the little kids running around on our street. I sat there and thought about it. "Of course not! I'm not graduating with someone four years younger than me!" She said, "Well, then do what you have to do in order to graduate and make the decision to put the work in to succeed." So with a pep talk from my mom and a second chance from my principal, I set a goal for myself, which was to improve my grades and stop putting out minimum effort and receiving minimum results. I had five months to prove myself and knew there was nothing that could hold me back—but myself.

I was never into what most of my friends and classmates were into outside of school, such as smoking, drinking, partying, or sex. And no matter what others were doing I was never influenced by their decisions because I knew who I was; I just couldn't find my rhythm academically. Once the goal was set I became focused only on achieving it, and I didn't have to worry much about cutting these negative actions out of my life because I never focused on them in the first place.

Once the last place on earth you would have seen me the year before, the library, became my second home and I used all the resources available to research projects and study. After school I would finish my homework as soon as I got home, which was a major improvement because in years before, I would let homework sit all night, sometimes for days, without touching it. If I had a project that was due in a week I wouldn't start to work on it until the night before or at my worst, the morning the day it was due. That was old me; the Cool Smart Kid had a positive attitude and completed his work on time.

The most unique and puzzling fact during this time was that I was technically not in a grade. I had to report to two homerooms in the morning because they didn't know how to place me. I was in school purgatory and it was the worst feeling of my high school years. I was either going to fail and remain in ninth, or succeed and continue in tenth, and both homeroom teachers were there waiting for me regardless of my effort and successes. At times, I was asked to attend assemblies for ninth graders and I never went because I was embarrassed. What made matters worse was that my first two report cards for the school year still read ninth grade. When report cards were issued at the end of the quarter students would share their grades with each other, especially if they got really good grades. Since middle school I dreaded this day because I never had good news to share and my friends always found a way to point that out on our way home. This year, even though my grades were improving there was no way I would share that I was still in ninth grade, so I used a black pen to write the number 10 over the number 9 so I could show others my report card.

Another obstacle that I had to overcome was the fact that since I did not have summer school for the classes I failed the year before, I had to retake them and I had a full schedule. During the winter I tried out for the basketball team again, but my focus and priorities were on making sure my grades were acceptable for the principal, and did not put much effort into making the team, ultimately not making the cut. I had to think about what was more important and realize that I had to cut some things out—and basketball had to be one of them. I went to one or two tryouts just to say that I went, but I stopped going the rest of the week and decided to stay focused on my grades.

The plan to improve my grades by the first half of the school year gave me tunnel vision because I cut out of my life anything that took away time from getting an A or B. I remained focused and worked extremely hard every week to improve my grades, even asking for extra credit when I got the opportunity. I made sure that I completed my work and did everything that I could do to make sure that I did not fail.

The ninth-grade and tenth-grade offices were right next to each other, and only a door separated the two. I was called down to the ninth grade office when our grades were entered into the report cards—it was time for the principal to see all of my grades. My palms were sweaty and I did not want to start sweating under my armpits because it might show on my shirt the rest of the day. I had become accustomed to chatting with the ninth-grade secretary because I had always been in the office for bad grades or detention. She looked at me and asked, "Are you sure you did well?"

"I hope so because I don't know what I am going to do if I am with you the rest of the year," I replied. The principal finally called me in and every grade looked good but there was one class that wasn't on her computer, math, since the teacher hadn't submitted the grade yet. She called the teacher to find out my grade. The conversation was probably two minutes but it felt like two days; I was so nervous that I did not pass the class. The principal finally hung up the phone and said "It looks like you got a C," and I went crazy in my mind. She said, "It looks like you did it and improved your grades enough to move onto tenth grade, so let's go to the tenth-grade office." She walked me two feet and said, "Now you are in tenth grade; good job!"

It's crazy how a couple of feet changed my direction. Opening one door literally changed my life. If I didn't change, I could have taken a different path. I headed back to class but all I could think about was that I completed the mission, I achieved the goal, and now I could hopefully continue to maintain this level of focus throughout the rest of the school year and leave this chapter behind.

One of the perks of being a student at Lower Merion was that every year Kobe Bryant would visit the school when the Lakers were in town to play the Philadelphia 76ers. The first time I saw him at school there was a crowd of students surrounding him, hoping for pictures and autographs as he moved through the hallways. I did not react as a fan but admired from afar how beloved and respected he was at his former high school. When I spoke to my dad after school I shared with him that I saw Kobe earlier in the day. He responded with an interesting question, "Did he get your autograph?" I laughed and said "No, of course not." He continued, "Well, why not?" I said, "Why would he want my autograph?" He responded, "You are made from kings and queens and you need to position yourself to where he is asking for your autograph and not the other way around." My dad saw so much potential in me and he always spoke to me like I was a star in the making.

When I turned 18 years old I told my mom I wanted a tattoo for my birthday. She drove me to South Street in Philadelphia to the same parlor she received her first tattoo. I asked the artist to write "The World Was Made For You" across my left arm so I could read it when I needed the motivation.

During my senior year I took a short story writing class. I needed this class to have enough credits to graduate on time, since my grades were so poor in ninth grade. This class was worth a half credit, but it ended up being my favorite class throughout high school because I got to be very creative and innovative, and develop my own stories and characters. As I graduated high school I didn't think much about writing stories as a career but it did spark my imagination and made me think about my earlier childhood days when I loved to write stories.

Chapter 4:

Faith and Perseverance

Once I graduated high school, I still didn't have any idea what I wanted to do and I was still working part-time at the same job I had during my senior year, at a car dealership washing cars. One night as I was sitting in the customer lounge I remembered watching a speech on TV being given by Barack Obama during his campaign for President. It hit me that I saw someone who I could identify with who was running for President and I became mesmerized by the size of the crowd he was speaking to. I began to evaluate what I wanted to do with my life.

Looking at the television screen I could see that I had more to offer than washing cars and working for someone else. After work that day, I drove to the library and checked out books written by Obama to read everything about his life. My mind began to shift from thinking small to having a sense of purpose, and I began to develop a vision of how I wanted to make an impact on others. I had a conversation one evening with my mom and said I have a vision of being a leader, and living life on my own terms.

Even if my mom never fully understood what my plans were, she never discouraged me from dreaming big and further encouraged me to write down my goals by asking me "Where do you see yourself in five years?" I created a vision board and I wrote down what I wanted to achieve. A few goals were to write a book, start a business, and become a community organizer and radio host. I chose writing a book because I had enjoyed the writing class I took so much and I knew I was good at it.

I kept writing story ideas after high school in my spare time and I had a vision of myself as a published author by the age of 19. It became clear from seeing how hard my parents were always working that I wanted to own my own business. There were days my dad couldn't get out of bed because he was so exhausted from work and I did not want to feel the same way as I got older. I didn't know what the business was going to be but I wrote it down as a goal. The goal of being a community organizer materialized because that's what Barack Obama was before he began his career in politics. I decided to write down running for political office because I assumed that would be the next step in helping more people after being a community organizer.

Lastly, I developed my interest in hosting a radio show. I don't know why but someone once told me I had a voice for radio, which was interesting because I also heard that if you have a voice for radio, you usually don't have a face for TV.

Now I had a vision of who I wanted to become and a plan to achieve my goals. It was time to call on my alter ego, because in order for me to achieve all of the goals on my list I needed to have faith in myself, be fearless, and have the perseverance to stay the course by working hard.

I moved on from the dealership to work as a landscaper for the summer, then work at UPS at the airport loading and unloading packages in the fall and winter. I worked the night shift and it was freezing cold during the holiday season. The coolest thing that I got to do while at the job was marshal out a plane onto the runway. It was a huge responsibility to help direct the pilot onto the runway for takeoff and at first I was worried I would forget the hand signals, but I made it through and the plane took off safely.

I was looking for a job that was closer to home so I left UPS for another car dealership in my neighborhood. Another valet there said to me he could tell that I was not going to be working there long because I always had something on my mind, thinking about bigger life goals. I was thinking about my short stories and how I just needed enough money to fund my goals.

I had a moment to myself in the back of the dealership one hot summer evening and I remember saying to myself, *There has to be more out there for me and I have to move on before becoming too complacent here.* So I left the dealership for another car company down the road.

A friend of mine had worked at this dealership for a number of years and I always wanted to work for Acura because I was very fond of their cars. Even though I moved from one dealership to another I needed to be around new people and not feel complacent by being at the same job for too long, especially when I needed to find the right work schedule to make enough money to pursue my goals. I worked at the dealership for a few months, until spring, and found another job as a landscaper at an apartment complex. When I left the dealership I knew that I was done working as a valet and closed that chapter of my life.

On the first day of the new job I immediately knew that I was not going to last long because it was not a good fit for me. I had worked as a landscaper before but this manager was very demanding and I did not have the patience to deal with the demands of the upkeep of the property. My mind was on bigger ambitions and I did not feel comfortable working there while pursuing my dreams.

I called the township and asked if they had any open positions for a summer landscaper and I filled out an application. Even though this was a similar position to the one I was leaving, I had a good relationship with the employees from working there in previous years and I would make more money over the summer. I received a call from the human resources manager who offered me the job as a landscaper two days before I received my first paycheck from the apartment complex. I notified the manager I was leaving and worked for the township all summer long.

One morning in the work truck I heard an announcement that the radio station was having a contest for a new program host. I was so excited because one of my goals was to become a radio host but I did not have any idea how I was going to make that happen. The rules of the contest stated that a contestant had to record a one-minute demo of themselves talking about a topic they were interested in, and send it to the radio station. If your demo was chosen you had the opportunity to host your own show for a day and each contestant would be judged by their performance. I could not wait to get off work and immediately get started on the demo. I found a camera that recorded audio that my dad had bought for me for Christmas and I began practicing.

My topic of discussion was education funding and the inequality of schools between rich and poor neighborhoods. I stayed up all night researching the topic and learning as much as I could before recording my demo.

Once I sent in the final version I listened to the radio every day hoping that my name would be called as a finalist. A week later I received a phone call from the station that I was chosen as a finalist and they gave me a date to come into the studio. I spread the word to all of my family and friends on the day I would be on the radio, and practiced every night what I wanted to say when I had my chance to be on air.

On the big day I made my way toward the station but I made a wrong turn and got lost. My cell phone did not have GPS and I relied on the directions that I wrote down on a piece of paper before leaving the house. I pulled over and asked someone for directions but I did not believe they knew where the building was, so I went with my gut the other way, and I ended up finding the radio station. I had wanted to get there a little bit earlier to calm my nerves and read over my notes, but I lost too much time.

Once in the office I was escorted into the studio and told that my show was going to start in five minutes. My palms sweated as I fumbled with my notes, nervously reading through my script as fast as I could. I looked out the window and took a deep breath, reminding myself that "I got this" and I was here for a reason. When the producer gave me the signal that we were starting I put the headphones over my ears. She pointed to me and said we are now live on air-and then something happened that I thought never would: I couldn't find my words and I completely shut down. I was not prepared enough to hold my own and host a show. The producer kept mouthing words to me to say something, anything, but the words just wouldn't come out and I felt so disappointed in myself that I was letting my family and friends down, those who believed in me and were listening.

The producer cut to a commercial. A full-time host for the radio station walked in and was prepared to take over the show if I did not get my act together. I collected my nerves and reminded myself once again that I was there for a reason and was going to finish strong despite my shaky start. When the commercial finished I began the second segment on a much better note and finished the show strong. The producer was very proud that I did not allow the other host to take over my show and that I found the confidence and courage to continue. I did not win the contest but I proved to myself that when I sought to achieve my goal, when I made a commitment, I would see it through to the end.

When the summer was over so was the position, so I needed to find a new job. On my way home one evening I noticed a "Now hiring" sign at a local pizza shop. I filled out a job application and soon began delivering pizzas, washing dishes, and cleaning the shop.

After a month I began looking for a new job and my mom told me that there was a new gym being built in our neighborhood and that a coworker of hers had a daughter who worked at a similar gym and I should check it out. She went on to say that the gym would be open 24 hours a day, seven days a week and I could potentially work there at night and work toward my goals during the day. I initially thought that was not a good idea because I've never set foot inside a gym, even though I was trying to work somewhere other than the pizza shop. I did not see the vision and I had no desire to work at the gym.

A few days later I was driving my car and got a flat tire down the street from where the gym was being built. There was a car dealership across the street from the gym and I walked to the dealership for help with my tire.

As I walked down the street I thought to myself, *Maybe there's a reason why I got a flat tire near the gym which leads me to walk past it* so I walked in and filled out a job application. Since the gym was still not open, I left the application in a folder, walked back to my car, and fixed my flat.

I became increasingly fed up with working at the pizza shop and frequently called the gym to let the managers know that I was interested in working there. After a week of persistent calling I was offered a position at the gym to work night shifts from 10 p.m. to 6 a.m. The job consisted of signing up new members to the facility, and cleaning while there were fewer members working out at night.

Now with a new job and a schedule that allowed me more freedom to pursue my objectives, I used the day to write my books and learn more about community organizing. I volunteered for local non-profit organizations and became a tutor for an afterschool program. My first leadership role was as vice president of the Ardmore Progressive Civic Association, which works to improve neighborhoods through volunteer work. During the monthly meetings I was able to meet with neighbors and hear their community concerns and figure out best solutions. A year later I was voted president of the civic association and continued in that role for two years. This position also helped me with public speaking because I never had to speak in front of more than a handful of people prior to running these meetings.

I remember the first time I spoke in front of about 10 people. I was so nervous and sweaty that I had to excuse myself and dry off in the bathroom, look in the mirror, and remind myself that I had the confidence to see it through. As each meeting went by I became more confident in my ability to speak publicly and these skills became invaluable as I pursued my career as an author, presenting to a large number of people.

On a cold and chilly Halloween eve I prepared to attend a retirement party for a local politician and mentor of mine. As I walked outside, snowflakes dusted my overcoat as it began to snow. I waited for the car to heat up when I realized I did not have a snow scraper for my windows and I wouldn't be able to see where I was going. Just when I thought I was going to be late for the party a truck pulled up next to my car, and a man wearing a jumpsuit, hat, and gloves approached my vehicle. He used his arm to wipe the snow off my windshield. I rolled my window down and thanked my dad for saving the day and expressed how happy I was to see him. He was driving home past my house and saw that I was in the car. I shared with him that I was on my way to the party and he was happy that I was staying focused and pursuing my interest. I gave him a fist bump while sitting in the car, told him I loved him, and drove to the party.

A week later on Election Day I volunteered for the first time, handing out flyers and literature outside my polling place, so voters were informed about the candidates before voting. I volunteered all day and learned much about the voting process and was intrigued about the integrity and commitment each resident had to vote as part of their civic duty and responsibility. When the polls closed in the evening I went home to eat dinner, changed into my work clothes, and walked to the gym to start my overnight shift.

I had so much on my mind after volunteering at the polls and thinking about my goal of running for political office, so after I made it to work I found time to call my dad and share a few of my thoughts. I expressed to him my interest in running for political

48

office one day. He offered words of encouragement as he always did, saying that I can do anything I put my mind to, that I was born to do great things, and that my mind was already where it needed to be, and with patience and hard work my body will catch up. Before we ended the conversation he reminded me of my tatoo that "The World Was Made For Me" and I was headed in the right direction. My dad said everything that I needed to hear in that moment and I was confident that I would find my purpose knowing he was proud of me and I had his full support.

A week later I was informed by my cousin that my dad had passed away due to a heart attack. I was devastated and crushed that my hero was no longer with me. My father instilled confidence in me at an early age and saw a vision in me that I didn't yet see. Since before I could walk he would tell me I was a king and born to lead. He pushed me to push myself to dream bigger, and believed that whatever I wanted to accomplish in life I could make happen. I was disappointed that I would never see my father again and I asked myself, "If he were here right now, what would he say to me?" I thought about it for a few minutes and responded, "He would tell me to keep my head up, stick my chest out, keep my boots laced, and keep marching on."

I made a commitment to myself from that moment on I would be fearless and relentless the way my dad saw me. Even though I preferred him alive and here with me, in a way, he died so I could live. He taught me everything I needed to know and now it was up to me to be the leader he saw in me since the day I was born.

I was ready to make more bold moves in my life and pursue my goals. I contacted an illustrator online to begin the process of creating my first book based on a short story about a newt named Newie with big dreams of becoming a Broadway singer, who takes an adventure to the big city to pursue his passion despite his father's wishes that he take over the family business. My dad used to call me New or

Newie when I was younger and I wanted to create a character that was fearless in pursuing his dreams like I was doing in real life.

I had a burning desire to run for political office to keep the promise I made to my dad, and I thought about how cool it would look to have my name on the ballot the same year Barack Obama was running for reelection. I created a political campaign plan, bought office supplies and a new suit, and knocked on doors all across the community asking neighbors for their signatures to put my name on the ballot on Election Day. There were many people who thought it was not the right time for me to pursue this goal and that I was too young and inexperienced. But they did not understand why I had to go through this process and so I continued to push and make a name for myself. A person who wants to run for state representative needs to collect the support of 300 registered voters – to write their names in support – and I missed the mark by only a few signatures. Most family and friends were extremely proud that I had the courage to run for office and I learned a lot about who really wanted to see me be successful and who did not. I held my head high and was satisfied that I was able to cross this goal off of my list, despite not winning.

I hung my suit back in the closet and focused on writing and publishing my first children's book. I did not have any experience publishing a book and would use a portion of my day to research the right way to do it. Midway through finishing the book, the illustrator's home in New York was damaged by Hurricane Sandy and he lost a lot of his possessions. I felt very bad for his situation and prayed that he and his family would fully recover. But I also thought that he may have lost the illustrations for the book we were working on, since a lot of his possessions were damaged by the water. He emailed me that his laptop was safe and that he could continue working on the book at coffee shops, lounges, or even his mom's office because he was as determined as I was to complete this project.

I compiled a list of literary agents and publishers to send my manuscript to in hopes they would be interested in my work and publish my book. I was rejected every time but I knew then in order to see my vision come to light, I had to put my destiny in my own hands and publish the book myself. The process took over a year because of minor setbacks and challenges but the book was finally published in January 2013. The story was not my best work but I proved to myself that I could publish a book and use it as a stepping stone to improve my writing, and a learning process for publishing my next book.

I had no reputation as an author so I reached out to local schools, churches, and other organizations to ask if they would be interested in buying my book and allow me to read it to their students. I received a lot of "nos" but I had already made up my mind that this was something that I wanted to do and keep pursuing, so I took advantage of anyone who said "yes" and used that as an opportunity to share my stories with children.

The next story I focused on publishing was called *Aron's Adventures*, about a young boy who loves science and technology.

The reader follows Aron on his quest for knowledge and adventure through exploring new inventions in a coloring and activity book. I did not see a lot of children's books with characters of color interested in science and technology, so I created Aron to address this need. I worked with a new illustrator and published the book in October 2013.

I continued working nights to make enough money to publish my books and build an audience. In February 2014 I published my third book *Newie: Big City Dreams*, as a sequel to the first Newie book. I wanted readers to follow Newie's next journey of adventure and the courage he showed to leave his small town to pursue his dream in the big city of New York. When children read *Newie* I want them to understand that not everyone will see his vision or talents, but he has to be courageous in pursuing his dreams no matter what people may think of him.

Now with three published books I decided it was time to take it to the next level and organize my first book signing. I called a local bookstore and asked if I could bring my books to the store and share my stories with the public and autograph my books. The bookstore owner was very nice – she had a passion for helping local authors – and we scheduled a day to set up my first book signing. I created a Facebook page and invited everyone on my friend list to attend.

I thought that this would be enough promotion to encourage people I knew to stop by and buy a book. When the day finally arrived the illustrator and I set our books on display as we waited for people to walk in the store. I had no expectations about how many people would come; I was just really excited to have my books in the store, knowing that a year ago I was starting out with just an idea, a pen, and paper. Only one woman came into the store and purchased a copy of my book. She said she was going to give the book as a gift to her grandchild. As we were packing up to leave I said to the illustrator to remember this day because there will be a time when we will create a book and there will be a line around the corner. This experience will not stop us but will give us the fuel to keep moving forward.

The next book I was compelled to publish that same year was *Believe in Yourself*, a book dedicated to a family member named Stephanie who passed away from cancer over the summer. The character was created in her likeness and the little girl in the book becomes too sick to trick-or-treat with her friends on Halloween. Her mother brings her a box of costumes and tells her that she will get over her illness as long as she believes in herself and stays strong.

As she tries on each costume she looks in the mirror and envisions what she can become as a healthy adult serving her community and the world. Stephanie helped build my confidence as I pursued my writing career and was the first volunteer to join me during a community project to rehabilitate a broken-down garage in our neighborhood. She truly did believe in me and I wanted to carry on that message to encourage all young people to be strong and confident, and believe they can achieve anything they put their mind to.

As I was working on a new story I thought about how I could use the knowledge that I have learned to publish my own books and help up-and-coming writers bring their creative works to life. I approached two friends from my neighborhood whom I believed would be a perfect fit for a poetry book, and had all the right qualities to become superstars if given the right tools to succeed. I asked them to send me their best material and I would help them publish their poetry. With no intention of making any money from their material, I published the book for them and guided them through the process so they could make money from their own book. It has been a pleasure to watch these writers grow and use their book as a calling card to reach and inspire countless readers of all ages.

Once that book was complete I set my full attention to finishing my next children's book titled *Aron Goes to the White House Science Fair*. The inspiration behind this book was that President Obama had established the first White House Science Fair, encouraging children around the country to create science projects that could potentially be chosen and viewed by the President in person at the White House. I thought this would be a fascinating story for Aron to develop a science project and highlight his trip to the White House Science Fair to meet President Obama! His science project is a time machine and he uses it to time travel with the President to meet Aron's favorite innovators, those who inspired him to become an inventor. The plan was for young people to see themselves as creators and innovators, especially children of color achieving high levels of success outside of sports and entertainment, not represented enough in books.

A year later I approached an important milestone on my journey, five years working nights at the gym while pursuing my writing career and my other goals. I would work eight hours a night until the early morning, then go back home to start my day. During the last five years I don't remember sleeping for more than six hours on any one night. I thought, *If I had more time during the day to focus on my craft and business, how much better could I be*? My dad used to tell me "Everybody wants to reach the top, but no one wants to climb the mountain."

I did my best to keep my spending in check and save enough money to invest in myself. After I paid my cell phone bill, rent, and car insurance, and spent only enough money to eat, I would have no money, sometimes struggling to pay for gas. It seemed like every month I didn't know if I was going to pay my student loan on time. I told myself that I couldn't live like this anymore and had to take a risk to improve my life. I told myself that I am fearless and I know what I have to do.

During the summer I organized another book signing at a different bookstore. This time I had a larger following and more published books. It was a blessing to go from having one person buy an autographed book two years ago, to now seeing a line of supporters waiting to meet me and sign their books. In the fall I published another story titled *The Journey of the Cool Smart Kid*, highlighting my poor choices in high school, and how I learned from my mistakes, found my purpose in life, and became the man I am today. This story was adapted for younger children to inspire them to remain motivated and focused on their education as they progressed through middle and high schools.

Once this book was complete I knew that it was time to take a leap of faith and stop working at the gym.

For five years I swept floors, cleaned dirty bathrooms, and lost countless hours of sleep because I was determined to succeed and I understood that this was a temporary job that would help make my dreams a reality.

I left with $800 in my bank account and the dream to be my own boss. I received a lot of help thanks to my mom and others who supported my dream. As I would share my bigger dreams and aspirations with people, some would project their fears on me by telling me all of the horror stories of pursuing one's dreams. I listened politely but with a grain of salt but trusted that the life I wanted would come with patience and hard work. When you're determined, the universe has a way of moving things out of your way and giving you what you ask for. My mom was nervous when I told her that I was leaving my job but has remained my most consistent motivator from the beginning of my journey. My mom saw a lot of friends throughout her life whose dreams never materialized so it made her a bit nervous that her son would take such a risk on a non-traditional path. I said to her one night that I could die tomorrow so why would I spend my time doing something that I don't want to do? I had made up my mind that whether I would become an author living in a mansion or living in my car I would live with the consequences and go for what I want.

I treat the universe and my surroundings the same way. I feel like I can get anything I want and I can attract anything I want. Anything that I see in my mind, I can hold in my hand. I had $800 when I left my job and I didn't know if I was going to pay my rent, pay my phone bill, or put gas in my car, but I knew it was going to work out. I knew my story was going to turn out the way it needed to, and I believed that God would continue to lead me to the right opportunities at the right times. With the right energy and positive attitude I was going to attract good people around me who would help me make a positive impact on the world and manifest any dream I dream.

During the early winter of 2017 as a full time author I decided to write and publish a new Aron's Adventures book titled *Aron Runs for Class President*. After a life-changing experience meeting his idol, Barack Obama, at the White House, Aron feels inspired to run for office at his school to create history of his own. I felt compelled to write this story because there are not a lot of African-American characters in books pursuing political office and every young person needs to see themselves as leaders in their schools and communities.

One evening during a networking event for authors and illustrators, I met an up-and-coming illustrator who lived close to my neighborhood. I expressed that I would love to work with her in the future and when I was ready to write my next book I would reach out to her. A few months had gone by and I was in a creative mood, ready to begin writing my next children's book, so I contacted the illustrator to collaborate on this project. In August 2017 I published my eighth book, *Where Did My Dream Go?* The inspiration for this book was that an early dream of mine in elementary school was to be an author. Through my transition years in middle and high school I lost my way academically and the dream began to disappear. When I had to make a choice about my future one of the questions I asked myself was where did my dream go? I wrote a short story based on that question, about a young girl named Jasmine who wakes up to find that she cannot remember her dream. Determined to find it, she searches for clues throughout her school day and in the process discovers something unexpected and exciting about herself. The lesson behind this story is that everything you need to be successful is already inside of you and when you have a dream that is worth pursuing, don't let fear stop you from chasing it.

Chapter 5:

Charity and Public Service Work

I seriously think I have an obsession with helping others. I'm always looking for ways to improve people's' lives and be of service to the world. I truly believe everything you put out into the world will come back to you, as I continue my mission of service to others. I am blessed with opportunities to grow in different aspects of my life that help me manifest my dreams.

Every day I would drive through my neighborhood and one day I saw a garage that was in desperate need of repair. It looked like it hadn't been touched in years; I couldn't tell what color the garage was originally, and the graffiti made it a true eyesore. I became fed up and decided that if no one else was going to make an effort to fix it I would do it myself. So I reached out to the owner of the home the garage belonged to, and expressed my interest in fixing the structure. The owner agreed that it was long overdue and made a commitment to buy a new door and paint to cover up the graffiti. I then called one of my biggest supporters, Stephanie, who is featured in the book *Believe in Yourself*, to ask if she would help me with the project. She went out of her way to buy paint and supplies, and we met at the garage, spending the morning painting it. Instead of waiting for someone else to improve the look of my community and complaining about it, I took action, rolled up my sleeves, and did the work myself.

One afternoon I stopped at the store for lunch and picked up a newspaper. When I made it back home I came across an article about a local TV station that was looking for fresh ideas for new shows, and anyone who may be interested in learning more about being a host should call the studio. Prior to reading the article I had no plans for the immediate future to be on television unless it was to be interviewed by the local news about a community project or book event. Never the one to turn down a great opportunity and learning experience, I called the studio and asked for a meeting to learn more.

The following week I walked into the studio and shared with the manager that I would be interested in hosting a storytime show for children. He seemed intrigued with my idea and gave me valuable insight on how to produce a great show. But by the end of our conversation it was clear that the station did not have the right equipment to produce the show I had envisioned. Once home I brainstormed new show ideas. I did not want this opportunity to slip through my fingers. I was a fan of PBS talk shows such as Charlie Rose and Tavis Smiley, mostly due to their interview styles and the depth of information they could elicit from their guests on a range of topics.

I came up with a new show idea, to interview local business leaders and up-and-coming artists. The difference between this show and others that I have watched was that I was interested in hearing about the journey of the guests more than what they had to sell. The name of the show would be *On the Rise*. I pitched this new idea to the station manager and he quickly approved it. Now that it was official that I was going to have a TV show, I began planning for potential guests and worked on marketing. A friend of mine who is a graphic designer created posters that I could use to promote the show online. I reached out to family and a few friends who are business owners and artists, to ask if they would be interested in being guests.

I had no experience hosting a show. For a week I watched a ton of seasoned professionals on late night television and studied their every move in front of the camera. When my first guest arrived at the studio I had no idea how this would play out, but I knew I had to look calm in front of my guest and not appear nervous. Once the camera started rolling I prayed that I did not mess up any of my lines, which I didn't. It certainly helped that my first guest was someone whom I've known for a long time and I was very comfortable discussing their upbringing.

I was so excited to complete my first show I went through my entire contact list to let everyone know the date the show would air. When I saw myself on the television screen for the first time I was at a loss for words. Just a few weeks back I was reading a newspaper and now here I was in my living room watching my own show with my mom and stepdad.

I would go on to interview more than 50 guests for my show over the next 12 months. The station manager gave me a chance and I took advantage of the opportunity. I'm always willing to try new things and push myself to greater heights.

When I started traveling to different schools to share my books, I felt disheartened to see schools in some communities with so few resources for their students. I would talk with teachers and parents who came to see me speak to their children about the basic needs of the schools. I thought that it would be a great idea to solve a common problem that I would hear often, the lack of parent-teacher communication. Wealthier school districts could purchase software and mobile apps to send information directly to parents, but underfunded schools still relied on sending paper flyers home, hoping they reached the parents. I wanted to create a mobile app to bridge this gap, but there was one problem: I had no idea how to get started.

I watched free online courses to learn more about mobile app development and researched local companies that could help bring my idea to life. When I found a company that was willing to help I shared with them my vision for the app. They gave me an estimate of how much it would cost and when I checked my bank account I was reminded that I might need a little bit of financial help to complete this project. I set up an online fundraiser and shared with family, friends, and peers that I was interested in creating a mobile app for schools and would love their financial support to help pay for the cost. I raised over $5,000 and paid developers to bring my idea to life. I called the app Let's Collab, and made it available on the web and for mobile phones.

Throughout my travels to different schools I shared the benefits of the app with principals and teachers, encouraging them to use it to communicate with parents. My heart was in the right place to address this issue but after a few months I put the app on hold to continue writing books.

Another thing that would bother me when I visited lower-income neighborhoods to read my book to a group of students, was I learned that the students don't have books to read at home. I began organizing book drives and asking businesses to become drop-off locations for customers to donate books, and I posted flyers on social media and local libraries to raise awareness of the campaign. Within two weeks over 1,000 books were donated and distributed to students in lower-income neighborhoods. I also created a pop-up library at a park where children and parents could "check out" a book to read in the park and then take it home.

Seeing the success of the first book drive gave me the confidence to organize more throughout the year and I enjoy the looks on kids' faces when they receive new books for the first time.

Another community project I established is an art workshop that benefits public school children. The idea of the workshop is to have children use their creativity to share the joy of art and reading with other children. One project is decorating home-library boxes that are filled with exciting, donated books and given to children who have no access to books at home. Art centers also collect gently used and new books at elementary and middle school reading levels to be used for the home-library boxes.

For Thanksgiving 2016, I wanted to do something different in my community so I organized a Thanksgiving dinner event at Bethel AME Church in Ardmore. I solicited donations from individuals and a corporate sponsor. The event was held on a Saturday afternoon a week before the holiday, and almost 200 families were served turkey and given a bag of food to take home.

The following year I decided to move the event to another location, this time an elementary school in North Philadelphia. Through a collaboration with the school and a non-profit organization, each student in kindergarten through second grade was read a book and their parents were recipients of turkeys. I heard testimony from parents being so grateful that they had received that Thanksgiving meal, and that if it were not for our efforts they would have had to go to a local food bank to eat turkey on Thanksgiving.

I organized storytimes at the local library and often invited police officers and firefighters to join me and read to the kids. The biggest draw was always the main event, when the children had the opportunity to play on the firetrucks and with the police sirens. When there was tension in a lot of communities nationwide concerning police and community relations, I would do my best to play a part in bringing people together by having children meet their local police officers in a non-intimidating environment, reading fun stories.

You never know who you may meet along your journey who can help you achieve even more goals. I had reached out to the township manager to see if he was interested in reading to kids for storytime at one of the libraries. He accepted the invitation and the day of the event there was a producer from the township to take pictures of his boss reading to kids.

We began chatting and he expressed an interest in recording a children's reading show at the studio. I replied that I had a similar idea when I hosted *On the Rise,* but it ended up not working out because the old studio didn't have the proper equipment. We finished the storytime with the township manager and that night I really thought about how it was perfect timing for the TV producer and me to meet at that library and discuss this idea of doing a children's reading show.

This was no coincidence. I emailed him before I went to bed and expressed that I wanted to explore this show idea with him. Within two months we put together a children's TV show called *Really Exciting and Delightful Stories,* which empowers young storytellers to find their inner voice and get kids to start writing and help them be more confident in presenting their creative work to a broader audience. We organized a writing contest to promote the program and encourage kids to write their own stories. I designed a flyer with all of the contest details and emailed almost every school in the greater Philadelphia area and beyond. For the first month I did not receive any submissions and began to think that no one would be interested in our show, but I kept sharing the flyer on my Facebook page and even recording 30-second promotional videos to add on our website. Within the last week and a half of the contest deadline we received over 20 submissions. The winning authors were invited to share their stories with me on TV and they loved every minute being the star of the show.

The program now hosts a series of writing contests throughout the year and has received submissions from all over the country.

I always believed we needed to do more with goal setting. During my school presentations in lower-income neighborhoods I began to ask students to imagine where they would like to live and what their community would look like, and then get them into that utopia world by asking, "OK, if you had all that, then where would you want to be? Where would you want to see yourself?" Just daydreaming in there, they could only think about their environment and what they saw. But I know some kids have a hard time visualizing this.

For some kids, I have to take them through an imaginary walk of life and ask them how they want it to be, and to tell me where they want to go in life. I think some of that is because of lack of exposure. Kids need to be exposed to more of life because you can't teach people something you don't know. A lot of kids don't know where they want to be because they don't know what is out there. There are kids who have never seen things outside of their neighborhood. There aren't enough programs that help expose our kids to enough diversity for them to even be like, "OK, that is possible."

People do more than work three or four jobs and drive for Uber. Our kids need to learn the concept of entrepreneurship. Part of that is developmental and I help kids to come up with ideas for a business, seek feedback from real business owners, and establish career goals. To begin the process of opening their minds to what is attainable I began to organize youth entrepreneurship workshops and invite business leaders as speakers. Kids can't say they are interested in being entrepreneurs if they didn't know what an entrepreneur is, looks like, and understands the hard work that is involved.

I was doing so many community events throughout the years that I thought it was a good time to set up my own nonprofit organization. The World Was Made For You, Inc. is a 501(c)3 that I formed to support children and educators in underserved communities, provide mentorship and creative-expression programs to youth, and provide young people a platform to become the leaders they were born to be. Through volunteering, education, and empathy, I believe all young people can create positive change within their community and beyond.

I named the nonprofit with the same words my dad would say when he wanted to remind me that I had all of the right qualities to be a leader.

I have been honored with awards for my commitment to inspiring our youth and supporting the underserved through charitable works in my community and beyond the region. Everything I give the world I do for the benefit of others, not for accolades or awards, because that comes truly from my heart.

Conclusion

During my childhood and transition years in school I found what I was truly made of. I was able to learn things about myself that I wouldn't have been able to in a traditional classroom setting. I embraced The Cool Smart Kid as an alter ego to get me through moments where I needed to reach a little further within myself and find the drive and determination to succeed. I built up the courage to keep going and the fearlessness to achieve my goals because I had a clear vision of what I wanted. I became The Cool Smart Kid when it was such a steep climb academically and I had doubts that I could overcome my obstacles, but I became fearless. Shortly after I graduated I was determined to succeed and do something larger than myself and I wrote down goals and developed a life plan. I again turned into The Cool Smart Kid and began pursuing my goals, becoming who I am today. As I think about my career as an author I'm always striving to push myself, push my limits for an increasingly larger audience, and push myself everywhere I go and in every step of my life. When I saw Barack Obama speaking in front of tens of thousands of supporters when he ran for President, I had a vision that I would do the same at some point in my life and inspire people, but I didn't know yet how I was going to do it. But I did see the future—that I would be a leader one day.

My vision became focused and unique to me as I developed my passion for writing children's books and empowering children through my personal stories. I then developed a plan to see the vision come to light. I had to be determined to succeed, to never give up, and to persevere no matter what. I had to be smart and know what was best for me. It's not just about being book smart but learning about yourself and finding what you are made of during tough times. I had to see myself in the future and not worry so much about the present, and understand the present was temporary.

On my journey I wasn't thinking about the jobs of sweeping floors, cleaning bathrooms, cutting grass, or being a cashier. Everything I was doing I felt was necessary at the time while I was making enough money to fund my dreams. Wherever you are in life, you need to develop a plan to see that vision come to life. Writing down my goals made my dreams real and I encourage you to take a piece of paper and write down all of your dreams and aspirations. Everything you want in this life, at any age, can be achieved, but it starts with a written plan because then it becomes real. You are saying to the world *this is what I want and I will not stop until I achieve it*.

But you have to take the first step. Even if it's just writing down what you desire on a piece of paper, you are moving in the right direction.

Along your journey there will be challenges. But if you think that you can't get through these challenges, remember that your inner Cool Smart Kid will get you through any obstacle. So that's why I want to share my life story and be a source of inspiration for others to take the first step on their path to becoming The Cool Smart Kid.

About the Author

Nahjee Grant is an award-winning philanthropist, motivational speaker, published author, TV personality, and celebrated storyteller who has shared his amazing life story to full-capacity rooms filled with people of all ages. But Nahjee's story wasn't always so glamorous. As a student, Nahjee was so unmotivated to succeed during his early high school days that he flunked out of ninth grade.

Fortunately, Nahjee was given a second chance to prove himself and soon began to see that he had a purpose in life. As a young man, he learned to combine his incredible talent as a storyteller with his passion for helping others. The result: a powerful, relatable story that resonates with people of all ages, races, and religions. Nahjee began sharing his personal journey of failure-turned-into-hope through his books and with local audiences, and quickly became a highly sought-out speaker. Today he travels to deliver his message of perseverance, hope, faith, and dreaming big. Nahjee's unique ability to connect with people has made a tremendous impact on the lives of countless men, women, and children.

In 2017 he founded the nonprofit organization, The World Was Made For You, Inc., which works to build bridges, inspire our youth, and support the underserved through charitable works in Philadelphia and surrounding regions.

www.nahjeegrant.com

www.facebook.com/iamnahjee

Become a Cool Smart Kid

I invite you to visit nahjeegrant.com to take the online course to help capture your vision and create a plan for your life. You can download the goal-setting workbook and watch the video at your own pace. Together, we will persevere and accomplish everything our heart desires.

Made in the USA
Middletown, DE
07 June 2022